# Crossing the Delaware

## George Washington and the Battle of Trenton

**Arlan Dean**

rosen central
**Primary Source**™

The Rosen Publishing Group, Inc., New York

Published in 2004 by The Rosen Publishing Group, Inc.
29 East 21st Street, New York, NY 10010

Editor: Eric Fein
Book Design: Michelle Innes
Photo researcher: Rebecca Anguin-Cohen
Series photo researcher: Jeff Wendt

Photo Credits: Cover (left), title page, pp. 6, 18 © Bettmann/Corbis; cover (right) illustration
© Debra Wainwright/The Rosen Publishing Group; p. 10 © Hulton Archive; pp. 14, 22 © North
Wind Picture Archives; p. 29 Courtesy of the Mount Vernon Ladies' Association; p. 30 Library of
Congress, Prints and Photograph Division; p. 31 Library of Congress, Geography and Map Division;
p. 32 Library of Congress, Rare Book and Special Collections Division

First Edition

Publisher Cataloging Data

Dean, Arlan
  Crossing the Delaware : George Washington and the Battle of Trenton / by Arlan Dean.
  p.  cm. — (Great moments in American history)
  Summary:  George Washington, commander of the Continental Army, surprises Hessian
  soldiers at Trenton, New Jersey, and leads the Americans in an important victory.
  ISBN 0-8239-4356-9 (lib. bdg.)
  1. Trenton, Battle of, Trenton, N.J., 1776—Juvenile literature    2. Washington,
  George, 1732-1799—Juvenile literature    [1. Trenton, Battle of, Trenton, N.J., 1776 2.
  Washington, George, 1732-1799    3. United States—History—Revolution, 1775-1783]
  I. Title   II. Series  2004

  973.3—dc21

                                                                      2003-008531

Manufactured in the United States of America

# Contents

*Preface*

The American Revolutionary War was fought between England and its thirteen American colonies from 1775 to 1783. The main cause of the war was the high taxes England placed on the goods used by the colonists. The colonists felt that the taxes were unfair and refused to pay them. British soldiers in the colonies were ordered to make the colonists follow England's laws, which included paying the taxes. This led to fighting between the colonists and the English soldiers.

The colonies' governing group, the Continental Congress, knew they would need a strong leader to command its army. On June 15, 1775, they picked George Washington to lead the Continental army. Washington had been the leader of the Virginia militia from 1755 to 1758.

Under Washington's leadership, the colonists had success in the early part of the war. However, by the summer of 1776, things changed for the worse. Washington and his troops were driven out of New York by British forces. Washington and his men retreated to New Jersey. By December 1776, Washington and his troops had set up camp in Pennsylvania. The weather was bad and the troops had poor supplies. Many of the soldiers' enlistments were about to be up. They would be free to leave the army.

Washington knew he had to show that the Continental army was a force to be feared. He decided on a surprise attack against British forces in the town of Trenton, New Jersey. Winning the battle would raise the spirits of his soldiers. However, if they failed, it could very well mean the end of the colonies' fight for freedom. George Washington knew he could not fail. . . .

The crossing of the Delaware River became part of American history and legend. Different artists pictured the crossing, each in his own way. This painting was done by Emmanuel Gottlieb Leutze. Leutze shows floating ice in the cold river, but there is no sign of the snow and rain that slowed the crossing.

## Chapter One

# THE ICY DELAWARE

*And so it begins*, General George Washington thought. It was the evening of December 25, 1776. He stood on the Pennsylvania side of the Delaware River, at McKonkey's Ferry. A soldier walked up to Washington. "Your boat is ready for you, General," the soldier said.

"Good," said Washington. When Washington boarded the boat, it rocked under his weight. Washington looked at his soldiers. Many were just teenagers. Before them, in the dark of night, was the Delaware River. Washington moved to the front of the boat. He addressed his soldiers: "The British have had us on the run for a long time. Now, it is time to give them a shot of their own medicine. We must take Trenton. We cannot fail. Our families and the colonies are counting on us."

Washington's words gave his men hope that they could win. The soldiers rowed the boat out onto the river. The river moved fast, carrying the boat toward New Jersey. The river was filled with large chunks of ice. Often, the ice would bang into the boat with a loud thud. A cold wind blew against Washington. He didn't let it bother him. His only thoughts were on the coming battle against the enemy.

When the boat reached the New Jersey side of the Delaware River, Washington got off. He stood at the edge of the river. There he watched the other boats of the Continental army as they crossed from Pennsylvania to New Jersey. The boats held soldiers, supplies, and even the horses. Some of these boats were called Durham boats. Durham boats were between forty and sixty feet long. They had been used to move items such as grain and iron up and down the river. Now, they were moving members of the Continental army. Washington had about 2,400 soldiers with him for this battle.

Washington took a seat on an empty box and watched the crossing. He tapped his foot on the ground uneasily. The crossing was taking too much time because of a sudden snowstorm. His plan was to reach Trenton before daybreak and surprise the enemy troops. The troops in Trenton were German soldiers working for England. The German troops were known as Hessians. Washington knew that the Hessians usually held a large party for Christmas. Washington chose to attack on Christmas, hoping to surprise the Hessian soldiers.

However, the last of the men did not reach the New Jersey shore until 4:00 A.M. the next morning. Washington knew he had little time left for a surprise attack. Soon, the sun would be up.

General Nathanael Greene (1742–1786) was thought by many people to be second only to General Washington as a military leader during the Revolution. In addition to his success at Trenton, Greene led American forces against the British in the Carolinas and Georgia.

## Chapter Two

# A CLOSE CALL

"Onward!" Washington shouted to his troops as he rode past them on his horse. The men were marching down the Bear Tavern Road to Birmingham, New Jersey. The weather had grown worse. A strong wind blew rain and snow into the men's faces. The soldiers struggled to keep up their quick pace. They suffered greatly in the bitter cold. Those without shoes left bloodstains in the snow as they marched.

Upon arriving in Birmingham, Washington split his troops into two groups. He and General Nathanael Greene led their group toward the Scotch Road path to Trenton. General John Sullivan and his group were sent directly south to Trenton along the River Road. Washington gave

Sullivan orders to halt the march for a few minutes so that both groups would reach Trenton at the same time.

Shortly after the two groups split up, Sullivan sent a messenger to Washington.

"General Washington!" called the young man as he raced forward on his horse. "I bring you news from General Sullivan."

Washington slowed his horse so that the messenger could catch up to him. "Yes, what is it?" Washington asked.

"General Sullivan says that his men's guns are wet from the storm. Many will not be able to fire."

Washington frowned and said, "This is bad news, indeed. But we cannot stop the attack. This might be our last chance to turn the tide of the war. Tell General Sullivan that if the guns do not fire, his men should use their bayonets. We must take Trenton. There is no other choice."

"Yes, sir," said the messenger, and he quickly rode off back to Sullivan.

During the long march, Washington shouted as he rode through the lines of men. "Soldiers, keep by your officers!" Wherever he rode, Washington fired up his men. He made them feel that they could do anything.

Suddenly Washington heard a shout from up ahead. He quickly rode forward. He found a small group of men walking through a field by the road. "You there!" Washington called. "What are you doing here?" Washington was surprised to hear that the men were soldiers from the Virginia militia. They had been assigned to General Adam Stephen's group. The men explained to him that they had been sent out by General Stephen to scout the area. They reported that they had just shot a Hessian soldier at a Trenton outpost.

Washington shook with anger. He feared that the shooting might have put the Hessians on alert. If the Hessians thought that the Continental army was in the area, Washington's surprise attack would be over before it even began.

The Battle for Trenton would not be the only time Washington and his troops would have to deal with very cold weather and poor supplies. This picture shows Washington's troops trying to stay warm during their time at Valley Forge, Pennsylvania. About 11,000 members of the Continental army used Valley Forge from December 19, 1777 to June 19, 1778.

## Chapter Three

# "YOUR COUNTRY WILL THANK YOU FOR IT"

The Americans had made good time on their march. They were fast approaching Trenton. As Washington made his rounds among the soldiers, he noticed a young soldier lying on the side of the road. The boy's feet were bare and bloody. Washington called to the boy, "You there, lad, get yourself up. Get back in the march before you freeze to death out here!"

The boy didn't respond to Washington. Washington swung down from his horse. He went over to the boy. Washington placed his hand on the boy's shoulder and shook him. "Wake up, soldier, you must keep moving."

The boy opened his eyes slowly and stared up at the general. He tried to stand but cried out in pain. "I'm sorry, sir, but I cannot walk. The ice and the

rocks hurt my feet too much," the boy said.

Washington called to a lieutenant who was walking by. "You, sir. May I have your scarf?" The officer took his scarf off without a word and handed it to Washington. Washington took a knife from his jacket. He cut the scarf into two strips. He handed the pieces to the lieutenant. "Tie them around the poor boy's feet so that he may walk," he ordered.

The officer did as he was ordered. "When we get to Trenton see that this boy gets a good pair of boots from the Hessians," said Washington. Then he leaned over to the boy and spoke softly. "You will make it, lad. Your family and your country will thank you for it." Washington patted the boy on the shoulder and leapt back onto his horse.

The Americans would soon be upon the Hessian outposts. Washington needed to be in the front lines to make sure everything went smoothly. On River Road, General Sullivan had stopped his troops for a few minutes as ordered by Washington. Sullivan wondered if it would

be enough time for Washington's group to catch up. He hoped for the best as he looked around at the soldiers. They were nervous but ready for battle.

After a few minutes, General Sullivan gave the orders to start moving again. The men continued their march down the road. Suddenly from the east, shots were heard. Sullivan noted with relief that the shots were coming directly from his left. This meant that his delay had been timed perfectly and that both groups were arriving at Trenton at the same time. Upon hearing the shots, the men walked faster.

The battle had begun.

This picture shows the surprised Hessian soldiers rushing to fight Washington and his troops.

## Chapter Four

# THE BATTLE BEGINS!

As the Americans approached Trenton, Washington saw an American man chopping wood in a nearby field. "Where are the Hessian guard posts in this area?" Washington asked the man. The man pointed to a small house about 200 yards down the road. Washington ordered his men take the house. At the same instant, a group of Hessian soldiers rushed out of the house. They began to fire at the American troops. Washington ordered the charge. The Americans began running at the Hessians. Those whose guns worked opened fire. The others used their bayonets as they attacked the Hessian soldiers. The Americans chased them into Trenton.

In Trenton, the sound of gunfire got the attention of some of the Hessian soldiers who were up early.

When he heard the gunfire, Lieutenant Jacob Piel ran to the home of Colonel Johann Rall. Rall was one of the leaders in charge of the Hessians in Trenton. Piel banged on Rall's front door. "Colonel Rall!" he yelled. "We are under attack!" There was no response from Rall. Piel used all his strength to bang on the door harder. The noise finally woke up Colonel Rall. He stuck his head out the upstairs window.

"What is going on?" he asked.

"The Americans are attacking us!" said Piel.

"I'll be right down," said Colonel Rall.

Piel waited nervously for Rall to get dressed. When Rall finally came out of the house, he was dressed in his uniform. "What has happened?" Rall asked.

"There has been gunfire near Pennington Road. I think the colonists are attacking."

"Calm down, Piel. The Continental army is nothing. They are just farmers and businessmen. If they come, all they can hope for is a good retreat. However, to be safe, let's take a look."

Rall started to get onto his horse but was stopped by the sudden boom of cannon fire. "Oh, no," said Rall. "They are already upon us. We must return fire! Get our cannons into position!"

As he rode off to oversee his troops, Rall was very worried. *I should have sent out a night patrol*, he thought. *If we lose today, it will be my fault for misjudging the Americans. They are tougher than I thought.*

About that same time, Washington was getting ready for his next move. He and some of his men were just outside of Trenton. He pointed to a small hill up ahead in the center of town. "Quick men!" Washington said to his officers. "Follow me with the cannons. We will set up on that hill overlooking the main streets of town."

In the town, the Hessians jumped into action, getting ready for battle. Carrying their rifles, they gathered to meet the American forces. On the hill above, Washington waited for just the right moment. . . .

The Battle of Trenton was brief but bloody—especially for the Hessians. Once they realized that they were outmatched, the Hessians gave up.

## Chapter Five

# THE VICTORY
# IS COMPLETE

"Fire!" Washington shouted to his men. The cannons blasted into the Hessians, catching them by surprise. At that moment, General Sullivan and his troops reached the main street. He brought his troops up behind the Hessians. The Hessians were now faced with gunfire from all sides. In addition, a heavy rainfall mixed with snow made seeing difficult. Unbelievable as it may seem, one of the Hessian leaders ordered their marching band to play. He hoped that the music would rally the Hessian soldiers. In the middle of the gunfire could be heard the sounds of bugles and drums.

Unable to get organized, the Hessians were forced to retreat. They broke into groups. One group ran to a field of apple trees just outside of town.

There, they made one last attempt to fight the Americans. It was too late, though. The Americans were everywhere. By then, the citizens of Trenton had joined the fight. They fired at the Hessians from the windows of buildings. The Hessians saw that their position was hopeless. They had no choice but to give up.

Another group of Hessian soldiers tried to escape. They ran across a creek at the edge of town. As they struggled through the icy waters of the creek, they were quickly surrounded by American troops. They too had no choice but to give up.

The Battle of Trenton was a complete success. The fighting had lasted about two hours. About nine hundred Hessian soldiers were captured. About one hundred Hessian soldiers were killed, including Colonel Rall. However, only four American soldiers were hurt. The Americans also captured food, clothing, and supplies. This was the kind of victory Washington and his men needed.

Later that day, Washington ordered his soldiers back to Pennsylvania. He did this because it was important for the day to end on a victory. If they stayed in Trenton, there was a good chance they would have to fight British soldiers sent to take back the town.

That evening, Washington spoke to his soldiers. He needed to change their minds about leaving when their enlistments were up.

"You fought today as brave and free men should fight," Washington said. Upon hearing his words, the men nodded to each other. "The soldiers that we defeated today are among the best the enemy has," Washington said. "I look at you all here tonight and feel great pride. I know that we can beat the British. And it is because of you all!"

The men cheered Washington because he had led them safely through a hard battle. Now, they all believed that they had a chance to defeat the British.

"This is the turning point, men." Washington continued. "We have been chased by the British for too long. This is our country. We have earned the right to be free. Yet we will have to continue our fight to be free. Freedom is worth dying for. Without freedom there is nothing at all!"

The men cheered for Washington. "Together we will win this war for America! Join me now for these reasons. Reenlist and send a message to England that we have just begun to fight. The king must now know that we will fight!" Washington said.

Again, the soldiers cheered Washington. And that night, a wonderful thing happened. All of the soldiers promised to stay in the Continental army and fight. They wanted to fight for their families. They wanted to fight for their colonies. And they wanted to fight for George Washington. They knew he would lead them on the path to victory and freedom!

# GLOSSARY

**attack (uh-TAK)** to try to defeat an enemy or capture a place where the enemy is

**bayonets (BAY-uh-nets)** long knives that can be fastened to the end of rifles

**colonies (KOL-uh-neez)** territories that have been settled by people from another country and is controlled by that country

**creek (KREEK)** a small stream, usually one that is larger than a brook and smaller than a river

**enlistments (en-LIST-muhnts)** when people join the army, navy, or one of the other armed forces

**Hessians (HEH-shuhnz)** German soldiers paid by England to fight the American colonists

**militia (muh-LISH-uh)** a group of citizens who are trained to fight but who only serve in a time of emergency

**outpost (OUT-pohst)** a military camp set up away from the main group of soldiers to guard against a surprise attack.

**retreat (ri-TREET)** to move back or withdraw from a difficult situation

**victory (VIK-tuh-ree)** a win in a battle or contest

# PRIMARY SOURCES

We can learn a great deal about the past by examining and analyzing different kinds of sources. Some of these sources include old letters, documents, maps, paintings, and photographs. The "Take Notice" flyer on page 30 is from 1775. It was used to get men to join the Continental army. By studying this flyer, we can draw the conclusion that using George Washington's name on the flyer would encourage people to join. The flyer also lets us compare and contrast how military ads have changed from the 1700s to the present.

Documents such as letters let us identify how people of the past felt about events of their time. The letter on page 32 gives us a look at George Washington's thoughts about the Battle of Trenton. Having this important letter lets us compare his report of the battle to other people's accounts. By comparing and contrasting Washington's letter to other reports, we can reconstruct this important historical event.

This painting of George Washington was done by Charles Wilson Peale. Peale painted this picture after the Battle of Princeton, which was fought on January 3, 1777. Peale was well known for painting the pictures of many American Revolutionary War leaders.

Flyers such as this one, printed in 1775, were used to get the colonists to join the Continental army. This flyer urges colonists to fight for the "liberties and independence of the United States."

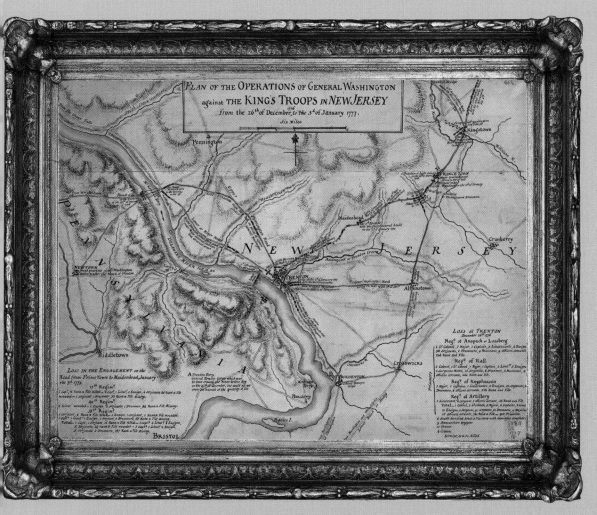

This map shows the placement of Washington's troops and British troops during the Battle of Trenton.

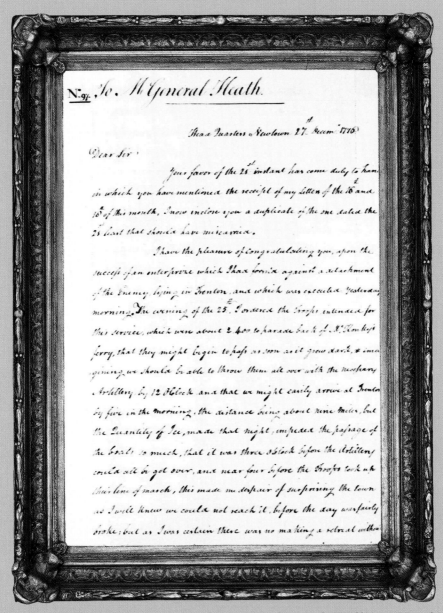

George Washington sent this letter to General William Heath. Washington wrote the letter on December 27, 1776. The letter contains Washington's report of the Battle of Trenton.